Amazing Planet Earth

EXTREME WEATHER

TERRY JENNINGS

W

FRANKLIN WATTS
LONDON·SYDNEY

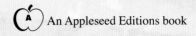 An Appleseed Editions book

First published in 2009 by Franklin Watts

Franklin Watts
338 Euston Road, London NW1 3BH

Franklin Watts Australia
Level 17/207 Kent St, Sydney, NSW 2000

© 2009 Appleseed Editions

Appleseed Editions Ltd
Well House, Friars Hill, Guestling, East Sussex TN35 4ET

Created by Q2AMedia
Editor: Michael Downey
Art Director: Rahul Dhiman
Designer: Ranjan Singh
Picture Researcher: Shreya Sharma
Line Artist: Sibi N. Devasia
Colouring Artist: Mahender Kumar

ISBN 978 0 7496 8807 3

Dewey classification: 551.55

All words in **bold** can be found in Glossary on pages 30–31.

Website information is correct at time of going to press. However, the publishers cannot
accept liability for any information or links found on third-party websites.

A CIP catalogue for this book is available from the British Library.

Picture credits
t=top b=bottom c=centre l=left r=right
Cover Image: Sean Martin/ iStockphoto.
Back Cover Image: Jim Brooks/ U.S. Navy

Insides: iStockphoto: Title Page, Celso Pupo/ Shutterstock: 4, Sampete/ Dreamstime: 5, Operational Significant Event in Imagery/
NOAA: 6, Debbie Larson/ NOAA: 7, Sergio Dorantes/Corbis: 9, Mike Theiss/Ultimate Chase/Corbis: 10,NOAA: 11, Rocco
Macri/123RF: 12, Danny Johnston/Associated Press: 13, Severe Storm Damage/ Associated Press: 14, Larry Atherton/Associated Press:
15, Vicnt/ iStockphoto: 17, Robert Spencer/Associated Press: 18, Jason Reed/ Reuters: 19, Christopher Morris/Corbis: 20, Christopher
Morris/ Corbis: 21, Armando Franca/Associated Press: 24, Li Xiaoguo/ Associated press: 25, Associated Press: 26, Ricardo Azoury/
Corbis: 27, Ben Heys/Shutterstock: 28, Kim Kulish/Corbis: 29, Shutterstock: 31.
Q2AMedia Art Bank: 8, 16, 22, 23.

Printed in China

Franklin Watts is a division of Hachette Children's Books,
an Hachette UK company.
www.hachette.co.uk

Contents

World's weather

Hot or cold, windy or still dry or wet, **weather** can make our lives pleasant or put us in extreme danger! Weather plays a big part in what we eat and drink, the type of clothes we wear and the design of our homes.

Wind and rain

The Earth's weather is powered by the Sun. **Winds** start blowing when the Sun's heat warms up the Earth's surface, causing hot air to rise and cooler air to rush in to take its place. Clouds form when water **evaporates** from the world's seas and oceans as **water vapour**. As these clouds cool down, their moisture falls as rain, **hail**, sleet or snow.

● Perfect, sunny weather for sunbathing on a Brazilian beach.

Wild weather

From time to time, severe weather strikes with deadly results. Long heat waves and **droughts**, sudden **hurricanes** and **tornadoes**, or freezing-cold **blizzards** and **ice storms** can bring large areas of a country to a complete standstill. Sometimes, weather conditions can be so severe that large buildings are reduced to rubble during an extremely violent **storm**.

● A heavy winter snowfall can cause massive traffic jams.

Hurricane Mitch

Hurricanes are huge, powerful windstorms that can be hundreds of kilometres wide. They form in warm and wet conditions, usually over an ocean near the Earth's equator.

Deadly hurricane

Hurricane Mitch struck Central America in late 1998. It was the most deadly hurricane to hit this part of the world for more than 100 years. Sweeping in from the Atlantic Ocean, Mitch lashed parts of Central America with violent winds of up to 290 km/h. A huge amount of rain fell, bringing devastating floods and **mudslides** to Honduras and Nicaragua. Mitch also caused ocean waves more than 6 metres high. The floodwaters reached the third floor of some buildings in Honduras.

Name: Hurricane Mitch
Location: Central America
Date: Oct–Nov 1998
Weather type: Hurricane
Fatalities: More than 11,000
Path of hurricane: Shown by the arrows on the map

• A satellite photograph of Hurricane Mitch. Around the calm centre of the storm are the hurricane's swirling clouds.

News Flash

BBC NEWS
November 1998

As Hurricane Mitch tore across Central America, the most deadly Atlantic storm in two centuries left a trail of destruction in its wake. About 10,000 are believed to have been killed, with Nicaragua and Honduras bearing the brunt of the storm. Development in some of the western hemisphere's poorest countries has been set back by as much as 50 years.

- Hurricane Mitch caused severe flooding. Parts of Tegucigalpa, the Honduran capital city, were buried under 12 metres of mud and water.

Human casualties

More than 3,000,000 people were badly affected by the hurricane. Many hundreds of thousands of people faced disease and poverty as their homes and workplaces were destroyed. Roads collapsed, crops were ruined and bridges and power lines were swept away. More than 11,000 people died as a result of the flooding and landslides, with about another 18,000 missing. The damage was estimated at more than $5 billion. Many months after the hurricane, the people of Central America were still struggling to rebuild their lives.

Life of a hurricane

A hurricane takes several days to form and is one of the most powerful of all weather systems. During a storm, the destructive winds spiral around a central, low-pressure area called an eye.

Strong winds

Hurricanes usually form over an ocean or a sea when the **temperature** of the air is higher than the temperature of the water. When this happens, water evaporates into the air and rises up, pulling in cooler air underneath. This movement of air leads to very strong winds that start to spin around the centre, or eye, of the hurricane. North of the equator, the winds rotate in an anti-clockwise direction. South of the equator, they turn clockwise.

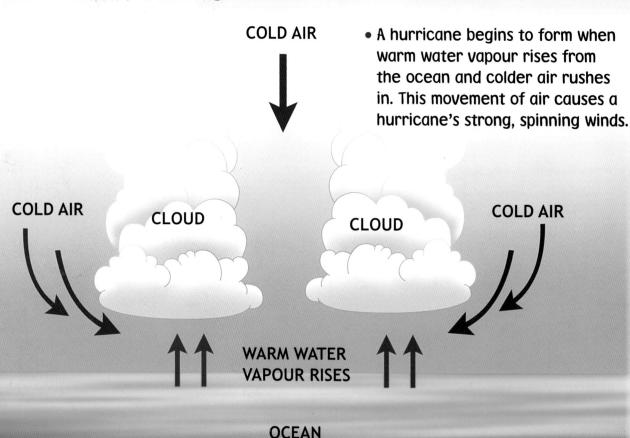

COLD AIR

COLD AIR

CLOUD

CLOUD

COLD AIR

WARM WATER VAPOUR RISES

OCEAN

- A hurricane begins to form when warm water vapour rises from the ocean and colder air rushes in. This movement of air causes a hurricane's strong, spinning winds.

• In 1988, Hurricane Gilbert caused gigantic waves that lifted this boat from the ocean and dropped it on land.

Hitting land

Some hurricanes die away before they reach dry land. Others get stronger and pick up more water as they move over a warm ocean. When a hurricane hits land, swirling winds can destroy buildings and huge waves pushed towards the shore can cause flooding. This movement of water is called a 'storm **surge**'. Once the hurricane is far away from the warm ocean, its destructive power soon dies away.

DATA FILE

• When wind speeds reach 120 km/h, a storm is called a hurricane.

• Hurricanes are given male or female names to help identify them, from lists drawn by the World Meteorological Organization.

• On average, most hurricanes last between three and fourteen days.

• **Global warming** may cause a lot more hurricanes in the future.

• North of the equator, the hurricane season usually lasts about four months, from July to October.

• South of the equator, most hurricanes occur between November to March.

Hurricane Katrina

When a powerful, swirling hurricane makes its way on to dry land from the ocean, it almost always causes a massive amount of damage. This is especially the case when the hurricane leaves large areas badly flooded.

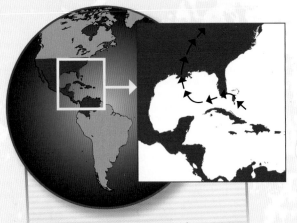

Name: Hurricane Katrina
Location: Southern USA
Date: August 2005
Weather type: Hurricane
Fatalities: More than 1,800
Path of hurricane: Shown by the arrows on the map

Developing storm

On 23 August 2005, an area of low **air pressure,** called a **depression**, developed above the Atlantic Ocean just north of Cuba. This depression was given the name Katrina when it turned into a storm. When Katrina reached the USA's Florida coast two days later, its winds had reached destructive speeds of up to 128 km/h.

● Hurricane Katrina's violent, spinning winds roared through the streets of New Orleans in the USA.

City flooded

After Hurricane Katrina had crossed over the warm waters of the Florida Everglades, it passed into the Gulf of Mexico. Here, the water temperature was a very warm 32 °C. This warmth increased the speed of the spinning winds in the hurricane, which gave even more deadly power to the storm. Hurricane Katrina hit land in the US state of Louisiana. The huge storm surges it brought caused vast amounts of water to break through the high banks, or levees, that protected the city of New Orleans. This led to sudden and severe flooding that killed many people in the city.

- **Thousands of homes were flooded in New Orleans when the levees gave way.**

DATA FILE

- A 'cyclone' is a hurricane that forms over the Indian Ocean.

- 'Typhoon' is the name for a hurricane that forms in the Pacific Ocean near the East Asian countries of Japan, China and the Philippines.

- The most deadly cyclone ever struck Bangladesh in 1970. It killed at least 300,000 people.

- When typhoon Saomai hit southern China in 2006, about 300 people were killed and 1,000 ships were sunk.

Terrible tornadoes

A tornado, sometimes called a 'twister', is a ferocious **whirlwind**. Although tornadoes do not usually occur in winter, there are always exceptions. In February 2008, a series of deadly tornadoes struck southern USA.

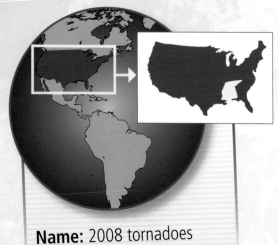

Name: 2008 tornadoes
Location: Southern USA
Date: February 2008
Weather type: Series of about 82 tornadoes
Fatalities: 59
Location of tornadoes: Shown by the yellow area on the map

Eighty-two tornadoes

In February 2008, huge thunderstorms lashed southern parts of the USA. These were triggered when warm, moist air that was moving north met a band of very cold air. Altogether, these thunderstorms produced about 82 tornadoes that affected a huge area. Many of these twisters brought destruction to densely populated areas in a number of states.

● In 2008, terrifying tornadoes ripped their way through parts of the southern USA, causing massive destruction.

Warning sirens

People awoke during the night to the sound of shattering glass and warning sirens. Horrified, those that could ran for safety, as tornadoes flung trailer homes into the air, flattened trees and factories and destroyed thousands of houses. In Macon county, Tennessee, an injured 74-year-old man, whose trailer home had been destroyed, was killed by another tornado as he waited for an ambulance to take him to hospital.

News Flash
Nashville, Tennessee
February 2008

Dozens of tornadoes sliced across southern US states ripping apart homes and shopping malls, killing at least 59 people and injuring hundreds more, officials said yesterday. Twenty-eight people were killed in Tennessee, 13 in Arkansas and seven in Kentucky, said officials in three states.

• A woman searches for personal items in the ruins of her house after tornadoes struck parts of the state of Alabama.

Disaster in Tennessee

The worst-hit state was Tennessee, where 28 people died. Some of these were victims of an explosion at a natural gas station where huge flames shot more than 150 metres into the air. Also in Tennessee, a shopping mall collapsed and a police radio tower was destroyed. This made it extremely difficult for emergency services to communicate with each other and rescue people trapped under rubble.

Students injured

At Union University, in Jackson, Mississippi, two living areas were destroyed, injuring many students. One student, who was playing pinball at the time, was pulled out of a building by the wind. Winds hurled him through the air while he was still holding the pinball machine.

Rescue work

In Shelby County, Tennessee, three people were killed when they ran for shelter to a nearby warehouse and the roof fell in on them. In many states, National Guard troops were called out to assist. Rescuers moved from house to house looking for trapped residents. Many people, some clinging to lengths of wood to stay afloat, were pulled out from swollen rivers. Fallen power lines and blocked roads hampered much of the rescue work.

• **Vehicles and buildings were wrecked by the destructive whirlwinds.**

DATA FILE

• The 2008 US tornadoes were the type that travel close to the ground for long distances of up to 80 km. These twisters are known as 'long track' tornadoes.

• Tornadoes do not normally happen in winter. The unusually warm weather that triggered the 2008 tornadoes may have been caused by global warming.

• Some of the hailstones that fell in 2008 were 11 cm in diameter.

• The USA's deadliest tornadoes occurred in March 1925. These left 695 people dead and more than 2,000 injured.

15

How tornadoes form

Tornadoes usually form from thunderclouds. Little or no warning can be given to the unfortunate people in their path because they appear very suddenly.

Tight funnel

Tornadoes often appear in groups, usually far inland, away from the ocean. They normally form during violent thunderstorms, when a hot, fast-moving, upward air current meets a cold downward air current. The hot and cold currents spiral around each other and form a tight funnel between a **cumulonimbus** thundercloud and the ground. This rotating column of air roars across the land, smashing objects in its path.

• Tornadoes are extremely violent rotating columns of air that reach down from a cumulonimbus thundercloud to the ground.

CUMULONIMBUS CLOUD

LIGHTNING

HOT AIR RISING

Trail of destruction

Smaller and much faster than a hurricane, a tornado can leave a trail of destruction 2 kilometres wide and 80 kilometres long as it rips its way along the ground. The most violent tornadoes have internal wind speeds of 480 km/h and can flatten large buildings, uproot trees and hurl vehicles hundreds of metres. Tornadoes can strike very quickly, but good planning can increase the chances of survival. Storm cellars in buildings have saved many lives.

- **Waterspouts** are similar to tornadoes, but form over water and are usually much weaker.

DATA FILE

- Tornadoes develop beneath huge thunderclouds that are produced along cold **fronts**.

- The most violent tornadoes occur in the USA. Here, there are about 1,000 every year.

- A violent tornado killed 160 people and injured 2,000 when it tracked through coastal villages in India in March 1998.

- In 1963, a tornado in north-west Assam, India, killed 139 people and left 3,760 families homeless in 33 villages.

- England has more tornadoes per square kilometre than any other country, but they are quite weak, so usually no-one notices them.

Freezing blizzard

Blizzards cause serious problems and can put people in danger. Heavy snowfall and high winds bring down power lines, leaving communities without electricity. Travel may also be impossible during severe blizzards.

Name: 2003 blizzard
Location: Eastern Canada and USA
Date: February 2003
Weather type: Severe winter snow storm
Fatalities: 27
Blizzard area: Shown by the yellow area on the map

Low temperatures

The crippling February 2003 blizzard in the USA and Canada was a record-breaking event. Major cities were brought to a complete standstill by the huge volume of snow that fell and by record low temperatures.

Ice and snow

The storm started in southern parts of the USA, bringing with it heavy torrential rain. As the storm moved north, temperatures dropped and water quickly turned to ice on the ground. Massive amounts of snow started falling across many cities. Some cities were covered with a layer of snow that was up to a metre thick. At times, more than 10 cm of snow was falling in an hour.

● Snow piled up on the streets of New York City enabled people to have a close-up view of traffic lights.

Schools closed

As the blizzard worsened, airports were closed and road travel was made absolutely impossible. People could not move about, and rescue services were severely hampered in their attempts to keep towns and cities functioning. In Baltimore, the roof of a railroad museum collapsed under the weight of snow, damaging many valuable engines. Most schools were closed for at least a week. With so much snow on the roads and nowhere to put it, some snowploughs were forced to push the snow into school car parks and playgrounds, causing even more schools to close.

• During the freezing conditions, de-icing liquid was sprayed on airport runways so that aircraft could land and take off.

News Flash

New York, USA
February 2003

In New York City, heavy snow and ice have made conditions very difficult. Airports have been closed, trains cancelled and streets made impassable to cars. Many pavements have been blocked by snow, so people are walking down the middle of the city's wide streets to get from place to place.

Deadly ice storm

When rain freezes as soon as it touches the ground, scientists call the result an 'ice storm'. In January 1998, one of the worst-ever ice storms hit Canada.

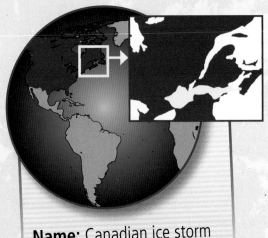

Name: Canadian ice storm
Location: Canada and northeast USA
Date: January 1998
Weather type: Freezing rain, ice pellets and snow
Fatalities: 28
Ice storm area: Shown by the yellow areas on the map

Freezing rain

For six days in January 1998, three storms of freezing rain and snow coated many parts of Ontario, Quebec and New Brunswick in Canada with up to 11 centimetres of ice. The freezing rain started to fall on Monday, 5 January 1998, just as many Canadians were returning to work after the Christmas holidays, and continued to fall for more than 80 hours. Usually, freezing rain lasts for only a few hours.

• **The weight of ice caused tree branches to snap and fall during the ice storms.**

Power failure

Heavy ice brought down power lines and telephone cables, forcing 600,000 people to seek shelter in hotels and hastily built shelters. Temperatures kept on falling, in places plunging to below minus 40 °C, and more than four million people lost their electricity supply. Freezing winds blowing from the Arctic chilled the air still further, killing thousands of cows. Millions of trees fell, and many more died during the rest of the winter.

DATA FILE

- During the 1998 Canadian ice storm, 28 people died, many from **hypothermia**, and 945 people were seriously injured.

- More than 130 massive electricity pylons were destroyed and about 30,000 electricity and telephone poles fell during the storm.

- Up to 16,000 Canadian troops were brought in to help clear up.

- Farmers had to dump about 10 million litres of milk as most milk-processing plants were shut.

- Most of the sugar maple tree plantations, which are used by Quebec's maple syrup producers, were permanently destroyed.

- It was the most expensive natural disaster in Canada's history. The cost of the storms was estimated at 5 billion Canadian dollars.

- Canadian Army soldiers work to repair power lines brought down during the ice storms, leaving many homes without heat or light.

Blizzards and ice storms

A covering of snow on the ground or a coating of ice crystals on trees can look attractive. However, there are times when heavy snow and ice can be deadly.

Snow formation

When water vapour freezes around dust particles in the atmosphere, tiny ice crystals are produced. These crystals gradually join together to form snowflakes, which fall to the ground when they are heavy enough. When thick snow, low temperatures and strong winds all happen at the same time, blizzards can occur. A phenomenon known as a 'whiteout' sometimes accompanies a blizzard. This is when heavy snow and low cloud make it impossible to tell where the ground ends and the sky begins.

• Snow formation

WATER VAPOUR FREEEZES INTO ICE CRYSTALS

ICE CRYSTALS JOIN TO MAKE SNOWFLAKES

• Blizzard formation

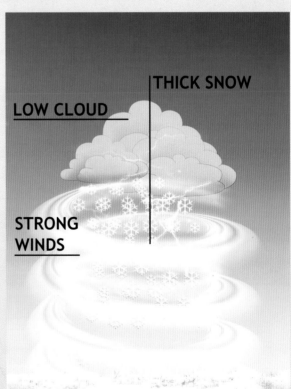

THICK SNOW

LOW CLOUD

STRONG WINDS

Supercooled droplets

In wintry conditions, when temperatures at cloud level are below 0 °C, or freezing point, water droplets that fall from clouds will be **supercooled**. This means they are likely to freeze as soon as they meet a colder layer below freezing point. When large, supercooled droplets fall on ground that is below freezing point, they spread out and freeze. This spreading out of ice quickly covers surfaces with a layer of ice that makes it difficult to walk or drive. The weight of this ice on overhead wires and tree branches is likely to bring them crashing down.

CLOUDS BELOW FREEZING POINTS

• Ice storm formation

SUPERCOOLED LARGE DROPLETS

FROZEN GROUND

Raging heat wave

Record high temperatures and a severe lack of rain were responsible for the deaths of some 35,000 people in Europe in the summer of 2003. Many of the victims were the very young and the elderly.

Raging fires

The summer of 2003 was probably the hottest in Europe in 500 years as temperatures reached 40 °C for more than 20 days. In the UK, the temperatures recorded were the highest ever. Weeks of heat and lack of rain had a devastating effect on farm crops throughout Europe, and thousands of cattle, pigs and chickens died. Fires raged in many European countries. In Portugal alone, 215,000 hectares of forest were destroyed by fire, an area the size of Luxembourg. Glaciers began to melt in Switzerland, railway lines buckled and road surfaces melted.

• An aircraft drops water on to a **wildfire** to try to put out the flames during the European heat wave of 2003.

Water shortages

The heat in 2003 caused severe water shortages and health problems. Rivers and **reservoirs** used for domestic water supply or to produce hydro-electric power either dried up or became dangerously low. In Serbia, the River Danube fell to its lowest level in 100 years, revealing bombs and tanks from World War II. In France, which relies on nuclear power for more than 75 per cent of its electricity, many nuclear power stations had to shut down. The river water they needed to cool their reactors had become too warm and the water levels too low.

- In 2003, a severe lack of water also affected China. Here, a farmer examines his maize crop, which was destroyed by drought.

DATA FILE

- In the UK, up to 300 died from poor air quality during the 2003 heat wave.

- The use of hose pipes was banned in many European countries.

- Railway companies set speed restrictions when temperatures rose above 30 °C. This was to avoid trains coming off the rails when lines buckled in the heat.

- Workers around Europe changed their working hours to avoid the worst of the heat. Dustmen started work earlier to pick up rapidly decomposing rubbish from streets.

- Some scientists believe that summers as hot as that in 2003 could happen every other year by 2050.

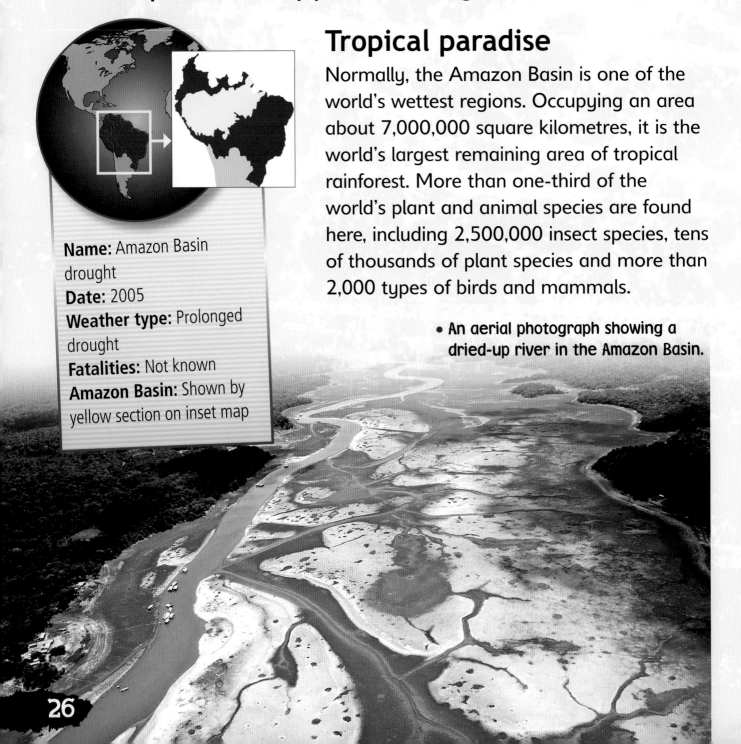

Severe drought

In 2005, a severe drought in South America's Amazon Basin left parts of the region extremely dry. Trees and crops withered, fires raged, fish died and deadly diseases spread to many parts of the region.

Name: Amazon Basin drought
Date: 2005
Weather type: Prolonged drought
Fatalities: Not known
Amazon Basin: Shown by yellow section on inset map

Tropical paradise

Normally, the Amazon Basin is one of the world's wettest regions. Occupying an area about 7,000,000 square kilometres, it is the world's largest remaining area of tropical rainforest. More than one-third of the world's plant and animal species are found here, including 2,500,000 insect species, tens of thousands of plant species and more than 2,000 types of birds and mammals.

• An aerial photograph showing a dried-up river in the Amazon Basin.

● During the drought of 2005, drinking water had to be taken by lorry to towns and villages in the Amazon Basin.

Worst drought

In 2005, the most severe drought on record blighted the Amazon Basin. Thousands of fish died and villages were cut off as waterways dried up. People were seen walking or riding bicycles in places normally used by canoes and riverboats. Large boats became stuck in mud, while forest fires raged as trees and other plants dried out. There was a severe shortage of clean water to drink and fish were no longer available to eat. Stagnant, muddy pools allowed malaria-carrying mosquitoes to breed rapidly. Even worse, the lack of water meant that raw sewage was not carried away, allowing deadly diseases, such as cholera, to spread rapidly.

DATA FILE

- The Amazon River drains a vast region, which is very nearly the size of Australia.

- Experts think that deforestation, or the clearing of large areas of forest, made the drought worse.

- The drought in South America's Amazon Basin was accompanied by a record hurricane season in North America.

- In the Brazilian city of Manaus, the level of the Amazon dropped 3m lower than average.

Power of the Sun

Droughts happen when there is no rain, or much less rain than usual, over a long period of time. Almost one-third of the Earth's land suffers from drought, affecting more than 600,000,000 people.

Cloudless skies

A heat wave is a period of very hot weather. In summer, if there are few or no clouds, the air and the ground is heated up by the Sun. The longer the sky remains cloudless, the longer the heat wave will last. People who do not protect themselves during a heat wave can become quite ill. Their hands, feet and ankles can swell up, and they may get bad headaches and feel sick.

● Reservoirs can dry up during a heat wave.

Using water wisely

Many countries around the world suffer from heat waves and drought. This is a problem that is likely to get worse in the future. Very hot temperatures can make droughts even worse. Sometimes, droughts can last for many years. When this happens, the land dries up and gets so hard that plants find it difficult to grow, even when it starts raining again. If we learn to use water wisely and try not waste it, some of the problems that are caused by heat waves and drought can be avoided.

● A raging wildfire sweeps towards beach homes and businesses during a drought in Malibu, California, USA, in 1992.

Glossary

air pressure the weight of the Earth's atmosphere pressing down on its surface

atmosphere the thick layer of air that surrounds the Earth

blizzard a very heavy snowfall accompanied by strong winds

cumulonimbus a large, billowing, flat-topped cloud that soars up into the sky. It is often called a thundercloud

depression an area of the atmosphere where the air pressure is lower than that of surrounding areas

desert a dry region with very few plants

drought an unusually long period of dry weather

equator the imaginary line around the centre of the Earth

evaporate when water is heated it disappears into the air as water vapour. It is said to evaporate

eye a fairly calm, clear area at the centre of a hurricane

front the forward edge of a mass of warm or cold air

global warming a general warming of the Earth's climate brought about by an increase of polluting gases, such as carbon dioxide, in the air. These gases reduce the amount of the Sun's heat that escapes into space

hail a type of precipitation that falls as pellets of ice

hurricane a swirling storm found in tropical parts of the Atlantic Ocean. Such storms are called cyclones or typhoons in Asia and willy-willies in Australia

hypothermia the gradual lowering of body temperature due to heat loss in cold weather. The person may become drowsy, fall unconscious or die if untreated

ice the solid form of water, formed when water freezes

ice storm a heavy rainstorm in which the rain freezes as soon as it touches the ground or some other solid object, the temperature of which is below freezing point

mudslide the movement of a mass of mud down the side of a hill or mountain

precipitation water falling from the clouds as rain, drizzle, hail, sleet or snow

reservoir a large, artificial lake used to store drinking water, produce electricity or to prevent a river from flooding

storm a period of violent weather. Storms usually have strong winds, dark clouds and heavy rain, hail or snow

supercooled water is said to be supercooled when it is cooled below its freezing point but does not turn to ice

surge a sudden rush of water

temperature the measure of how hot or cold something is

tornado a very violent whirlwind. A tornado is called a twister in the USA

tropics the regions near the Equator that have a hot climate all the year round. They lie between the Tropic of Cancer in the north and the Tropic of Capricorn in the south

waterspout a tornado over the ocean or sea

water vapour the gas or mist that forms when water is heated

weather how hot or cold, wet or dry, still or moving the air is at a particular time

whirlwind a strong wind that whirls around or blows in a spiral

wildfire a fire that burns grassland, forest, scrub, bush or other wild plant life

wind air moving from place to place

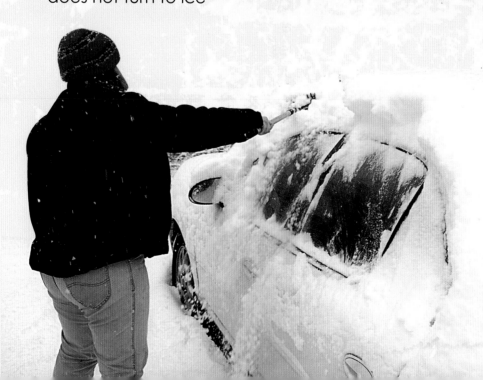

Index

Webfinder

http://geography.about.com
A wide-ranging and easy-to-use website providing information on world geography and climate change. This site also includes a section dedicated to maps

www.drgeorgepc.com
This website provides a wealth of information on tsunamis, earthquakes, volcanic eruptions, hurricanes and storm surges

www.fema.gov/kids/dizarea.htm
A child-friendly website listing a wide range of natural disasters and how to take steps to survive them

http://weather.about.com
A comprehensive website packed with information on the world's weather, including how we forecast the weather. This site also includes lots of quizzes and projects for children